Survival in Youth Ministry

Survival in Youth Ministry

Robert J. McCarty

Saint Mary's Press
Christian Brothers Publications
Winona, Minnesota

To the young people of St. William of York Parish in Baltimore, who have been my touchstone in youth ministry, keeping me "real" and "honest," and who constantly energize me with their enthusiasm, their faith, and their love of life.

To Shannon, my favorite young person and my daughter, who has uniquely challenged me to be the kind of adult that ministry with young people requires and who is my reminder that youth ministry does work.

To Maggie, my wife, friend, and co-minister, who loves and cares deeply for young people and who is my role model for relational ministry with teenagers.

To my colleagues in youth ministry in all their varied settings, who share a passion and commitment for this vocation and for whom youth ministry is not just a job, but a worthwhile adventure.

The publishing team for this book included Robert P. Stamschror, development editor; Cheryl Drivdahl, copy editor; Gary J. Boisvert, production editor and typesetter; Jayne L. Stokke, Romance Valley Graphics, cover designer and cover illustrator; pre-press, printing, and binding by the graphics division of Saint Mary's Press.

The scriptural quotations contained herein are from the New Revised Standard Version of the Bible, copyright © 1989 by the Division of Christian Education of the National Council of the Churches of Christ in the United States of America, and are used by permission. All rights reserved.

The displayed quotes on pages 22, 24, 27, 28, 29, 31, 32, 33, 34, 35, 46, 48, 49, 50, 51, 52, 53, 54, 55, 56, 65, and 66 are from a private, unpublished survey conducted by the author.

Printed in the United States of America

Printing: 9 8 7 6 5 4 3 2 1

Year: 2002 01 00 99 98 97 96 95 94

ISBN 0-88489-317-0

Contents

Introduction

Survival sounds like a very harsh word, especially when used in conjunction with *youth ministry*. What could be better than working for God? and with young people? Youth ministry is perhaps the most exciting and challenging ministry in the church today—just ask any youth minister. But as more and more people choose it as a vocation and a career, an alert should be sounded that the average tenure for a professional youth minister is not very long.

According to the *New Parish Ministers* study conducted by the National Pastoral Life Center, youth ministers have the shortest occupational life span among all parish ministers: over one-third stay in the field one year or less.[1] Even when remaining in the profession, youth ministers may rank just behind migrant workers in length of time in one place.

Something happens to a person after taking a position in church ministry. That "something" is not always positive or healthy—and youth ministers are especially subject to it. As rewarding and exciting as youth ministry can be, survival is a critical issue today for many people serving in it.

Many enter this ministry with very high aspirations and hopes but leave feeling disillusioned, bitter, and angry. Some even have their faith shaken by their ministry experience. The *New Parish Ministers* study stated:

> [Of all ministers,] youth ministers seem to derive the least satisfaction and support. The full-time youth ministers find ministry the least affirming, their co-workers the least affirming, their supervisors the least satisfied, parishioners the least satisfied, and youth ministers are least likely to encourage others to enter this ministry. While the number of youth ministers in our sample is rather small—just seventy-three—the consistency of their responses makes us think that this ministry needs particular attention. (P. 102)

Yet, I am convinced of the personal, professional, and spiritual value of ministry in the church, including youth ministry. Having worked in professional youth ministry for the past twenty years, I not only have survived it, but continue to be excited, challenged, and grateful for the opportunity to minister to, with, and for young people. My purpose in writing this book, therefore, is to explore with you problematic characteristics and conditions of youth ministry and to share the strategies and practice that I, and others, use not only to survive youth ministry, but to enhance it. In other words, the purpose of this book is to answer the question, What can we do to maintain the enthusiasm, excitement, energy, and sense of call that initially attracted many of us to youth ministry?

To answer that question, I will do the following:

▶ Describe the effect of professionalism, power, and authority in the church on our experience of youth ministry.
▶ Identify some of the myths that pervade our ministry.
▶ Examine the tensions, conflicts, and frustrations that affect longevity in our ministry.
▶ Describe patterns of spiritual health, along with ways to foster it.
▶ Offer practical strategies for surviving in youth ministry.
▶ Provide self-reflection exercises for assessing and improving our survivability.

My Perspectives

This book is written from the viewpoint of several perspectives that I hold about adults and youth ministry. These perspectives greatly color my approach to and understanding of the survival issue in youth ministry.

We, as adults in youth ministry, tend to be experience rich and language poor. You and I are very rich in the experience of youth ministry. We all have our stories of successes and failures, of frustrations and joys, of young people and programs. But most of us seldom reflect on these experiences in order to learn from them. Sometimes we don't have the words or the language to articulate these experiences so that we can benefit and learn from them. Hopefully, this book will provide both the opportunity to reflect on and the language to articulate the experiences you've had in ministry, and thereby enable you not only to survive, but to gain more enjoyment from, this challenging ministry.

Even though ultimate answers for survival issues in youth ministry are not always possible, we must raise these issues to make survival a clear and prominent objective. To call attention to survival issues is not to be pessimistic about either the ministry or the church. Rather, awareness of the problem is the first step in any change—and is a first step in survival. So, to seek awareness of survival issues in youth ministry can be a healthy, optimistic, and hopeful sign for the ministry.

We tend to resist change, even change for the good. An honest reading of this book may challenge long-held perceptions, attitudes, and ministry styles, which we can actually influence and control to make positive changes. To survive, we may need to view our ministry differently, redefine our roles, and reset our priorities.

Survival in youth ministry, then, needs to begin with an honest assessment of our ministry, with its frustrations and problems as well as its blessings and joys. Hopefully, this assessment will alert us to the aspects of our ministry that need to be challenged and changed, and provide the awareness needed to consider behaviors, attitudes, and approaches that foster a healthy experience of ministry.

I do not pretend to have all the answers for all the issues and situations confronting youth ministers today. Situations are so varied and issues so individual that claiming solutions that work in every instance would be foolish. However, it is vital that we begin to define, discuss, and respond to the elements affecting healthy participation in ministry.

Format

This book utilizes a workbook format. Each chapter first discusses particular issues affecting survival in youth ministry and then, at the end, provides reflection questions and worksheets for applying key insights and learning to your own situation. Much of the content of the chapters is based on my experiences in parish and diocesan ministry and my conversations with volunteer and full-time youth ministers, and on the results of a private, unpublished survey I conducted of professional youth ministers from across the United States. The survey asked these questions:

> ▶ When you first started in youth ministry, what did you do *right?*
> ▶ When you first started in youth ministry, what did you do *wrong?*
> ▶ What recommendations would you give someone just starting a youth ministry position?
> ▶ What are some key issues and concerns affecting your survival in youth ministry?

The survey comments were anonymous, and I have interspersed some of them in the following chapters, both within the text and displayed in dark boxes. I am very grateful for their honesty and insights, and for the commitment to youth ministry that they reflect.

Suggested Use

For individuals, reading the book chapter by chapter and doing the reflection exercises at the end of the chapters might be the most helpful process. However, it may be a more valuable experience if two, three, or even a small group of people read the book together. For people who have already begun to network for mutual support, sharing, and prayer, this book can be a great help in giving direction and structure to that effort.

Audience

This book was written with professional youth ministers primarily in mind. However, what is perceived in the terms *professional* and *youth ministers* needs to be more clearly described.

Professionals are not only salaried or stipended youth ministers. Professionals are all people, salaried or not, who have ministerial competence in, along with responsibility for, significant aspects of a youth ministry program in a particular setting. Given this perception, many volunteers who serve as youth ministers in various settings are regarded as professionals. This perspective is further defined in chapter 1.

The generic term *faith community* in this text refers to the parish, school, or diocese, or any other level or dimension of community in which the church is ministering to young people.

Therefore, youth ministers include coordinators of youth ministry programs, parish youth ministers or advisers, school campus ministers, retreat team members, catechists, coaches, those involved in outreach programs, diocesan youth officers, and all others ministering to young people.

So, the audience for this book consists of any paid or volunteer staff person with responsibility for youth ministry. The new minister as well as the seasoned veteran will find the material valuable, though each will read through the eyes of their experiences.

Finally, though this book is written from the perspective of youth ministry, the survival issues and skills described here will be valuable for those in all church ministries, since many experiences are shared in common.

Reflection: Your Story

①> Take some time to remember how you came to be involved in youth ministry.

    a. What was your experience of church (or youth ministry) during your teen years? How did this affect your decision to get involved in youth ministry as an adult?

    b. As an adult, who called you to youth ministry? How did you first get involved? Did a particular person first invite you into this ministry? Who? What gifts did that person see in you for this ministry?

    c. Why did you first become involved in youth ministry as an adult?

② Now take some time to reflect on your situation in youth ministry today.

   a. What gifts or talents do you now bring to this ministry?

   b. Why do you now choose to do youth ministry?

   c. For how many years have you been involved in youth ministry? For how many more years do you expect to stay? Why?

   d. What issues, concerns, or problems threaten your survival in youth ministry?

Professionalism, Power, and Authority

Three permeating issues greatly affect our experience of ministry in the church: professionalism, power, and authority. These are subtle and often unseen elements in situations, relationships, and conditions that create tension, conflict, and frustration in youth ministry. Recognizing and understanding them is a large part of surviving and thriving in youth ministry.

Professionalism

Though *A Vision of Youth Ministry* was written and set national standards for Catholic youth ministry in 1976,[1] youth ministry is one of the newest professional ministries in the church, especially on the parish level. When compared historically with the development of ministry in the church in general, fifteen or twenty years is, indeed, not very long. And as a young ministry in the church, youth ministry finds that it still needs to prove itself. Building up its professionalism—articulating a clear vision of the ministry, and identifying and advocating for the competencies and standards integral to the ministry—is an ongoing need.

We must be proactive in taking responsibility for our ministry as a profession and for ourselves as professionals. To be proactive means to take the initiative in creating vision and direction and in setting professional standards for it. In doing so, we begin to "own" our ministry and profession.

In the introduction to *Competency-Based Standards for the Coordinator of Youth Ministry,* published in 1990, the National Federation for Catholic Youth Ministry (NFCYM) stated:

> By issuing national standards for youth ministry personnel, the NFCYM is giving direction to the future of youth

ministry, as well as rewarding and affirming those persons already working in youth ministry for their formation efforts. By proposing and approving these standards, the NFCYM is ensuring the quality of its profession and is promoting professionalism for qualified persons.[2]

Here, the NFCYM is challenging all those involved in youth ministry to achieve a professional level of competence. Being competent is not only necessary for the good of the youth to whom we minister, but is also necessary for our own survival.

The standards document is "must" reading for everyone working in youth ministry, whether as salaried or volunteer professionals.

Characteristics of a Profession

John Roberto, the cofounder and director of the Center for Youth Ministry Development, offered four distinctions to help further recognize the effect of professionalism on youth ministers.[3]

"A profession can be an occupation or vocation." For all of us, youth ministry is a vocation—a calling. For some, it is also an occupation—employment providing a livelihood. But it is as a vocation that we consider youth ministry to be a profession. Consequently, whether involved in youth ministry as salaried employees or as nonsalaried volunteers, by way of our vocation, all of us are challenged to be professional and to meet professional standards.

"A profession requires formal education in the knowledge and skills particular to that field." The growth in training opportunities and programs on local, diocesan, college, and national levels points to a commitment to enhance the professionalism of the youth ministry—a commitment we all need to take on.

"A professional has assured competence in youth ministry, which implies standards for competence and methods for evaluating competence." Youth ministers, as professionals, need to assure constituents and clients that they are competent in their field. The NFCYM's competency standards are a valuable tool for both identifying necessary competencies and evaluating development in the knowledge and skills for effective youth ministry.

"Professionalism is primarily an attitude or style." Professionalism should be more about being part of a group known for its trustworthiness and credibility than about salary and benefits. To achieve this character for youth ministry, we must embrace professional standards and levels of competency, knowing that these not only enhance credibility, but also enable us to be better ministers. On the other hand, to continually enhance our skills and knowledge also creates a valid position from which to discuss just salaries and benefits.

As Roberto further pointed out, professionalism is not a status conferred vertically, from *above*. Professionalism flows from the "'horizontal authority' of our ministry colleagues, of our diocesan ministry organizations, and of national ministry organizations for professional standards and support for professionalism in Catholic Youth Ministry" (pp. 1–2). Consequently, professionalism is within our grasp. We need not depend upon higher powers to achieve it. We are as responsible for the professionalism of youth ministry as we are responsible for our survival in it. In fact, professionalism and survival in youth ministry go hand in hand.

In regard to survival, establishing professionalism in our ministry is especially important for dealing with the issues of power and authority that often arise. Professionalism enhances personal power and, in doing so, makes more possible a respectful relationship with authority and authorities.

True power and authority are givens that arise out of interactions between people. People cannot genuinely exercise them in a unilateral way, though some attempt to do so through use of force. This raises the question, How are power and authority defined and perceived in our experience of youth ministry?

Power

Power derives from relationships between people and is rooted in personal self-esteem and dignity. Power is best defined as the ability to act. It is our ability to effect or prevent change in our life, such as to make decisions that influence our life goals and our lifestyle, or to take advantage of opportunities to enhance our personhood.

The two primary models of power are power-over and power-with. Power-over seeks to dominate and control others, whether in personal relationships, in ministry, or in the larger society. Power-over is frequently experienced negatively, often flows from the top down, and tends to elicit violence, divisiveness, isolation, enslavement, and abuse. It is competitive and aggressive, used by persons who see their needs, hopes, visions, and goals as more important than others'.

Power-with is creative, dynamic, and nonviolent, flowing from a recognition of and respect for the giftedness of others. Power-with fosters community and personal growth, and respects the dignity of others. Power-with seeks to relate rather than win. It fosters collaborative relationships in which everyone is able to meet their needs, share their gifts, and live out their vision.

Empowerment—allowing people to exercise their power—is the result of power-with. Much as Jesus empowered the Apostles to make the important decisions in their life and affirmed their personhood and dignity, we should empower the young people and adults with whom we minister.

Power is operative wherever two or more people are gathered. In our ministry, we are always interacting and working with a variety of people—pastors, principals, staff, parents, young people, and so on—so power is always an issue. The challenge is to minister from a model of power-with, a collaborative style that truly empowers others while allowing us our own power.

With regard to the power issue in youth ministry, our task can be seen as threefold: to claim our power (to enhance our self-esteem), to share our power (to create a community), and to use our power (to build the Reign of God). In the process of claiming, sharing, and using our power, we are actually being proactive in our survival. Accepting our personal power allows us to take the initiative in determining the direction of our life, to accept responsibility for our actions, and to make important decisions. We begin to feel real power when we finally realize that we always have a choice, even if it is a choice of attitude.

This proactive stance toward power in youth ministry contrasts markedly with a victim-and-reactive approach. In the victim approach, we give our power away. And in being reactive, we blame others for problems in our personal and ministerial life, making these problems the fault of someone else, rather than accepting responsibility for them. The victim-reactive youth minister may consider every problem, obstacle, or tension to be the fault of the pastor, hierarchy, principal, staff, or parents. The victim-reactive person probably has real difficulty with authority of any kind, even legitimate authority, projecting all responsibility and power onto the person or persons holding that authority. If we operate from a victim-and-reactive stance, we are accepting a power-over model—and we assume that the person holding authority has all the power. Then we feel as if we have no ability or responsibility for changing difficult situations. In this state of being, survival in youth ministry is highly unlikely.

Authority

Authority is the process by which patterns of power are sanctioned. It is a product of negotiation between people. As with power, we can be proactive in dealing with authority—setting the criteria of when and to what extent legitimate authority can direct our life and our ministry. Being proactive with authority means accepting legitimate authority where appropriate and resisting illegitimate authority where it attempts to control our life.

Legitimate authority is coextensive with responsibility. For example, the pastor is responsible for the parish, the principal for the school, and others for their defined area of ministry. They all have legitimate authority in their realm of responsibility. As youth ministers, we are given responsibility for the community's ministry to young people and have a right to the legitimate authority that goes with that responsibility. To be proactive, we need to claim that authority and to collaborate, or work with, those whose authority crosses through or umbrellas our sphere of ministry. We overstep authority when we exercise it as a power-over relationship, failing to recognize or respect the personal, professional, or ministerial gifts of others and the legitimate authority that goes with responsibility.

Some people have a misguided image of authority figures—tending to have false expectations of them. Some consider higher authorities to be the most knowing, most skilled, and most gifted in the community, as well as more fair, more moral, and more faithful than the rest of the community. This tendency sets up two traps. The first trap is having such unrealistic expectations of those in higher authority that disappointment and frustration are inevitable. The second trap is projecting all responsibility onto those in higher authority, making ourselves responsible for nothing. Seeing authority figures as godlike allows us to forgo responsibility, since we can say, "I am not as good or talented as those in positions of higher authority, so I can't be as responsible for my actions." This pattern of avoidance not only fosters feelings of inadequacy, but also destroys our legitimate authority and often includes inappropriate criticism of those in positions of higher authority. Throwing rocks, verbal and otherwise, at those in authority is a victim-reactive approach to the issue of authority in youth ministry, and is hardly conducive to survival in it.

The task in dealing with the issue of authority is to assess honestly our relationship with all those that have authority over us in our ministry setting, and to assess equally the relationships in which we are the authority.

Being proactive in the issues of professionalism, power, and authority is crucial for surviving in youth ministry. Maintaining competence in the ministry, accepting responsibility for it, and claiming, sharing, and using our power and authority to carry it out can be the difference between surviving and not surviving.

Reflection: A Self-Analysis

① Consider all the different tasks and roles that constitute your position in youth ministry: planning, budgeting, doing a newsletter, and so forth.

a. List the top ten skills you use in your ministry.

b. Write each of the following codes beside the appropriate skill:

S = your strongest skill
W = your weakest skill
F = the skill you use most frequently
D = the skill you find most difficult to use

c. List other skills you would like to develop.

d. Pick one of the skills you would like to develop. What are some of the ways you could learn this skill? Of these possible ways, which is the most practical one? Can you do this? Will you do this? When will you do this?

2. Vocation and occupation are easily intertwined in youth ministry. When does your ministry most feel like an occupation?

3. Having a comprehensive understanding of youth ministry facilitates its implementation. What aspect of youth ministry do you need to know more about?

4. When it comes to authority in youth ministry, which do you experience more often, vertical or horizontal authority? Explain.

5. What is one practical thing you could do to further your sense of professionalism in youth ministry?

Myths

Myths are part of our "collective unconscious." They lie right beneath our consciousness and function as lenses through which we perceive, understand, and interpret the world. They shape our view of ministry and our vision of our role in that ministry. Their effects are found in our attitudes, expectations, and assumptions about the church and the ministry, and the way we participate in them.

When what we see, understand, and do by way of a myth does not match reality, we are operating with a false myth. False myths often are the cause of frustration, tension, and depression simply because our experience of our world is not how we assume it should be as a result of those myths.

In youth ministry, and in church ministry generally, false myths must be identified if we are to stay psychologically, spiritually, and even physically healthy. False myths must be identified if we are to survive.

False Myths in Our Ministry

At least five false myths operate among youth ministers.

The church is fair. Justice is an integral part of church teaching. But in many gatherings of church ministers, it is common to tell favorite stories about the insensitivity and perceived hypocrisy experienced in working in the church. These negative stories seem to come forth readily, suggesting the frequency with which they happen as well as the need for support in dealing with them.

Though the church is filled with well-intentioned people trying to live its mission and ministry, even well-meaning people make poor decisions and choices at times, leading to conflict, tension, and even anger.

The problem is that the myth that the church is fair leads us to expect church agencies to be more just, more fair, and more sensitive to their employees than we might expect other agencies to be. Making complaints about government or big business comes easy. Often, we even expect those organizations to be insensitive to the needs of people. But the church? No! And this perception is especially likely when ministry is a person's first "real" job.

If we take a true close look, we find that church authorities, even those with seminary or graduate education, often have little or no training in staff development or staff relationships, or for dealing with employees. Also, many clerics in positions of authority have little experience with the pressures and concerns of lay workers today. They have limited understanding of the costs of health care, raising children, or maintaining a home. It really is a myth to see and expect the church to be more fair than any other agency.

The church owns my soul. "I work for Jesus, and therefore my time and energy should be dedicated to him and the church in this extremely important ministry." The myth that the church owns our soul readily supports becoming a workaholic, because we never have enough time or energy to do the ministry as well as we want, or as the myth suggests that we should.

An important step in exposing this myth is looking to Jesus and examining the style of ministry he modeled. He seemed to take quite a bit of "time off." Perhaps authentic ministry doesn't require "giving up our soul" for the church. In fact, it's probably more accurate to say that church ministry should enable us to "save our soul," rather than burn it out.

Also, consider what we are modeling to young people when we work eighteen hours a day, seven days a week, fifty—or fifty-two—weeks a year. And what are we leaving behind for the person who follows us in this position? Who would want to follow us!

This issue of developing a healthy understanding of what ministry requires from us in terms of time and energy is further addressed in chapter 4.

Youth ministry is not a job, it's a vocation. This myth flows from the previous one. We sometimes fail to understand vocation as a total life commitment, in which work, including ministry work, is only one aspect. If the notion of vocation is restricted to our ministry, we begin to work harder and longer. Ministering becomes ingrained in our lifestyle, and soon we aren't able to identify where our work ends and our personal life begins.

> I had to remind myself that my job does not equal my entire life!

If we identify our vocation with only our ministry work, we soon forget to take care of the important relationships in our life. We don't take care of ourselves physically, emotionally, relationally, or spiritually.

It is easy to rationalize this myth by saying: "The kids come first. My ministry is who I am. I have to be about this work!" Like most rationalizations, each of these statements has a grain of truth, but when the grain becomes the whole truth, the myth is in charge and our survival is in jeopardy. Then we fall into the deadly traps of failing to take time off, of feeling that we can't ever leave the work, of being always "on." We need to remember that we could work every hour of every day of every week, and we would still *not* be able to meet all the needs of our young people. Our ministry is not intended to meet all our young people's needs because it's not *our* ministry alone. Youth ministry belongs to the faith community, and perhaps our real vocation lies in a faith-filled, healthy, whole-life living of the Gospel.

The church is a democracy. This may be the most recognizable and obvious myth. However, we still sometimes fail to recognize that the church is a hierarchical institution, modeled on a monarchy, and usually slow to change. The church doesn't usually make decisions and exercise leadership according to any expectations this myth might suggest.

In the governmental style of the church often experienced in youth ministry, the pastor is usually authoritarian by training. This approach to parish leadership even fits with the expectations of many parishioners, especially those who grew up with a Father-is-always-right syndrome. What makes this myth particularly conflicting is that youth ministers are usually young adults, especially in the early years of their career, and developmentally may still be acting out against authority and pushing for immediate change. When this myth is paired with this type of person, the tension and frustration can be especially explosive.

Many models of institutional leadership exist, including hierarchical, centralized, and shared authority. Our parishes, schools, and other varied ministry settings will reflect these different models. All of them are valid. All are effective in the appropriate situations. We need to identify the model of leadership used in our ministry setting and determine how to change, adapt, or accept the reality.

Everyone thinks youth ministry is important. This myth may be the most difficult to uncover and confront. Though it is true that ministry to young people is often given high priority in polls and surveys of parents, parishioners, and parish staff, in many parishes it continues to suffer from an inequitable allocation of staff, money, resources, and physical space or facilities. In many cases, a significant contributor to this dichotomy is a limited understanding of youth ministry. Many people see the parish's or school's primary role in this ministry to be educating young people in the doctrine and tradition of the church—the *what,* or content, of faith. Though this role is important, by itself it is a very narrow understanding of youth ministry. Advocating for funding for a comprehensive approach to youth ministry is difficult when most don't see beyond a religion class. Expanding the vision of youth ministry is a critical task of the youth minister.

Coupled with this narrow understanding of the scope of youth ministry is the common perception that any youth ministry position other than teaching is an entry-level position. This perception challenges comprehensive youth ministry to prove its credibility. And that's okay. Recall that a recognized dimension of youth ministry today is the need to establish itself as a profession with standards and competencies. We need to be advocates for the ministry, especially in our own setting.

Further, even though most will verbally support the need for youth ministry, we have to remember that not everyone likes teenagers. Frequently, local convenience food stores display a sign that says Only Two Teenagers Allowed in the Store at a Time. As joyful and faith filled as teens can be, they can also be rowdy and even intimidating. But is there any more crucial work today than with our young people?

> I had great difficulty establishing youth ministry as a fully recognized department and not just the "stepchild."

Having been exposed and named, these myths may now seem obvious. That is good. But unless they are consciously clarified and identified, these myths can subtley have great influence in shaping our perception of our ministerial role and be a threat to our survival in this ministry.

Reflection: Myths and Your Ministry

1. Review the myths identified in this chapter.

   a. Which of these myths affect your perception of your ministry?

   b. Do other myths affect your ministry perception? If so, what are they?

   c. Which myth or myths are dominant in your ministry setting (parish, school, diocese, community, other)?

   d. Which myth or myths seem to be dominant for your supervisor (pastor, principal, program director, other)?

② Sometimes we ourselves contribute to these myths in our ministry. Do you perpetuate certain myths by your approach or style of ministry? Explain.

③ Which myth most needs to be debunked, or exposed as false, in order to enhance your survival in youth ministry?

④ What would change about your approach to youth ministry if the myth in question 3 were debunked?

⑤ What first step could you take in order to reveal the truth behind the myth in question 3?

Longevity

How many youth ministers do you know who have been in their position for over three years, and how many do you know who have left before their third year? The pressure, frustration, and anxiety that can develop within the first three years can become overwhelming—enough so to cause us to rethink our calling. It usually takes three years to develop a comprehensive approach to youth ministry. And along with the actual task of developing the program are the added tasks of adjusting to the parish staff, fitting into the parish structure, and enabling the parish community to create a vision for its ministry with youth.

Longevity Factors in General

According to a survey of over one hundred youth workers, conducted by Dr. Mark Lamport of Gordon College, those who have left youth ministry cite thirteen major reasons for doing so:
- Burnout: 76 percent
- Lack of results: 49 percent
- Inadequate pay: 29 percent
- Staff conflicts: 27 percent
- Spiritual stagnation: 26 percent
- Inadequate training: 20 percent
- Inability to adapt to the ministry setting or culture: 18 percent
- Uncertainty of God's call: 18 percent
- Marital disharmony: 18 percent
- Promotion: 13 percent
- Illness: 13 percent
- Too old: 11 percent
- Fired: 8 percent[1]

Although some do leave the ministry because of one particular issue, for many the decision to leave is based on a combination of a number of these factors. For example, according to the *New Parish Ministers* study, 73 percent of youth ministers "think that there may come a time that they will no longer be able to afford to keep working in the church."[2] Further, the study revealed that youth ministers often don't find the satisfaction and support necessary to keep them in ministry, and that the almost complete availability young people expect of them dooms them to early burnout (p. 95).

Longevity Factors in Particular

Survival in youth ministry is greatly enhanced by identifying the factors that are unique to our situation and particularly affect our stay in this field. Though these factors often overlap and are joined with others, they can, for clarity, be discussed separately. Let's investigate some of them to see if any particularly apply to us and if so, what can be done to deal with them.

Staff conflicts: Whenever two or more people work together in a common setting, some conflict is going to arise. However, people in church ministry especially seem to be unwilling or unable to confront and manage conflict. This tendency, rather than the reality of the conflict itself, makes staff conflict in youth ministry threatening to survival.

I was only twenty-one when I accepted my first position as a parish youth minister, and I was far too idealistic in many respects. There were some real personality conflicts in the staff, and I lost an awful lot of respect for the pastor and one other staff member in the process. Not that I should have become suspect by nature or even pessimistic, but I certainly needed to lower some of my expectations of other people.

Staff conflict can arise from a variety of causes: competing needs and goals, hidden agendas, poor interpersonal communication, poor staff communications, and more. Have you ever had to fight for meeting space for your program? Or have you ever had to compete for time on the office computer and copy machine? Working with a staff should be a source of support, but for many it becomes a source of tension and frustration.

Conflict is a reality. Even the Apostles were reprimanded by Jesus for arguing over who would sit on his left and on his right. Rather than direct all our energy toward building a conflict-free environment, we need to develop skills for conflict management and establish an attitude that accepts conflict as a potential source of energy and even growth.

Though it is not possible, or desirable, to eliminate all conflict, much of the negative kind can be reduced by a collaborative, rather than competitive, style of ministry—a style rooted in the realization that we are all working to carry out the church's mission to build the Reign of God.

Confusing expectations: Just how much agreement do you think you'd find about your job description? Are you and the rest of the parish working from the same vision of youth ministry? We often get caught between what the pastor wants and what the parents want and what the young people want. Confused and conflicting expectations about our job and about the program's outcomes can quickly undermine support and trust.

> The pastor was not very supportive of the program and really didn't understand young people. I feel I didn't at that time know how to handle the situation, especially because for him it was always numbers [of youth attending programs].

Conflicting or ambiguous expectations about roles and goals can also lead to difficulties, misunderstanding, and disappointment in relationships.

An important step here is to take the time to discern the implicit or assumed expectations that key people have about our role in the parish and about the goals of our ministry. Though this is easier to do at the hiring or beginning stage of our ministry in a place, it should in any case be done as soon as possible. Much frustration can be avoided by clarifying assumptions and working toward mutually agreeable expectations.

> I gave in to unreasonable expectations. I tried to please everyone and considered it my fault if all parties were not completely satisfied.

Clearly written job descriptions are essential if we are to avoid the trap of conflicting expectations. However, job descriptions often tell us *what* to do in our ministry, but not *how* to do it. The *how* of ministry also can be subject to differing expectations. In addition to the *what* in a job description, a list of standard operating procedures that clearly explain how the staff is to work might be very useful. Examples of these procedures include how supplies are ordered, how items are placed on staff meeting agendas, how announcements get into the weekend bulletin, how rooms are reserved, how meetings are arranged, how financial records are kept, how office hours are established, and on and on. Clarifying these procedures not only reduces differing expectations, but will make job descriptions more complete and more easily implemented.

> Get all the real expectations out on the table. If the parish has not done the proper groundwork in educating the parish community about the need for or vision of youth ministry, then this should be of primary concern. Hold off on programming until there is more support than an arbitrary cash figure on a budget sheet.

Adding to the potential of conflicting expectations, people in youth ministry often find themselves constantly changing roles. At one time or another, sometimes simultaneously, a youth minister is expected to be a program planner, budgeter, newsletter editor, counselor, prayer leader, coach, trip leader, and resident expert on youth. Giving these roles proper and due priority according to the circumstances involved is a difficult but necessary task, especially if we are also spouse, lover, friend, parent, and unique person.

Developing clear job descriptions, identifying operating procedures, and setting role priorities will go a long way toward clarifying confusing expectations and will prevent much of the frustration and misunderstanding that results from them.

Lack of support: Have you ever taken a ministry position and suddenly found yourself all alone? Have people said or implied, "You're the professional, you do it"? Have you heard people who have been working in the program breathe a collective sigh of relief signifying that now someone else is going to handle everything?

Feeling alone with the youth ministry in the parish is discouraging. We need the support of other ministerial staff members, the parents, and the young people themselves. We have to be honest, though, about the unspoken or unconscious messages that we might be sending to the staff and the parish. If we are sending signals that the ministry belongs to the "professional," then people might think their support is not needed or wanted. If, however, we clearly define our role, expectations, and needs, we have a better chance to involve and gain the support of the community—and that's good ministry. The key is to build slowly. Only do the ministry for which you have the necessary support, resources, and time.

Another dimension of this issue is the opportunity for support from our peers in the ministry. People in ministry need to come together for personal, professional, and spiritual nourishment. Gatherings and organizations of youth ministers are spreading rapidly on local, diocesan, and national levels. Finding or developing such support groups helps youth ministers maintain continued health. Chapter 5 will address the issue of support groups more fully.

Difference of vision: A difference of vision has its strongest effect when it exists within the ministerial setting in which we are working. Does my vision of church fit with the vision of the people in the parish, school, or diocese? Do we share a common understanding of church ministry? of the role of youth in the church? of youth ministry itself? Just as there is a difference between a narrow sense of youth ministry and a comprehensive one, there can also be significant differences about what youth ministry is to accomplish. Is it supposed to empower young people as the young church of today, or to provide young people with entertainment and supervision? Is it to call young people to responsible participation in the church, or to simply pass on the facts of faith so that they can be better-informed adult Christians? What does the parish, school, or community want for its young people?

How do we come to a shared vision of youth ministry? One youth minister in the survey stated it this way: "We must be able to gently lead people toward a new vision." Perhaps *gently* is the key word here. And maybe we can begin with those already involved in youth ministry.

Youth ministry belongs to and is the responsibility of the faith community. It is not *our* ministry, and it is not the *youth's* ministry. Another youth minister in the survey said, "I immediately began to establish a core group of teens and adults to expand the vision of youth ministry for the parish beyond my personal vision." Part of our role, then, is to advocate for a comprehensive and shared vision of ministry to young people.

Lone Ranger approach: Do I see youth ministry as *my* ministry, and I am suppose to do it all? Or do I see youth ministry as *my* ministry, and you are invited to help me implement *my* vision of it? Either way, this is the Lone Ranger approach to youth ministry.

The Lone Ranger approach can be a form of empire building. Our particular constituency becomes a clique within the larger community, fostering a "guru" style of ministry. Everything becomes dependent on the youth minister.

> I really didn't train adults or have them as an integral part of the program, which meant everything fell on my shoulders and if I was sick, something had to be canceled.

The Lone Ranger approach also narrows the breadth of the ministry, because the range of possible programs is dependent on the youth minister's time, experiences, and talents.

> I did not spend an adequate amount of time to develop a foundation of leaders—I assumed too much in the beginning. I placed too much initial emphasis on programs, rather than on nurturing ministers who would then be far more effective in program development.

Further, the Lone Ranger approach is an invitation to burn-out ("I have to do it all—or die trying"). It can also lead to even more serious issues. When the involvement and presence of other adults is lacking or nonexistent, the young people themselves tend to become the youth minister's peer group or primary means of support, creating an unhealthy situation for both the youth minister and the young people.

Fortunately, the Lone Ranger approach is an issue over which we have control. Our approach to youth ministry flows from the way we see our role in it. And seeing through the Lone Ranger approach reveals that youth ministry is most effective as a team effort. Teamwork creates the structures and leaders that enable the ministry to expand and continue even if the youth minister leaves. Actually, a critical test of effectiveness is what is still in place six months after a youth minister leaves. If the ministry goes with the minister, it has, to a large extent, failed.

Again, we need to be mindful of the language we use when referring to the youth ministry program. Do we often use "I," or "we" when speaking about the program? Do people hear "I need . . . ," or "We need . . ."? The plural is the language of an inclusive ministry, denoting ownership and participation by other adults and young people.

And how do we refer to our position? If we are listed in the parish bulletin, what is our title? Is our job title *youth minister,* or *coordinator of youth ministry?* The first implies that the entire ministry is ours and formalizes the Lone Ranger approach. The second says we coordinate the community's ministry to youth and projects the image of a team approach. The title *youth minister* can set us up to be scapegoats. Either the community expects us to do everything or we expect us to do everything. So when things go wrong, it's our fault. And, of course, when things go well, it's our doing. The title *coordinator* signifies that the ministry flows from the mission of the faith community and belongs to the community. Therefore, the community, with the guidance and direction of the coordinator, is responsible for the effectiveness of the ministry.

Projecting a negative image: A major source of tension and frustration can be the way we deal with the difficult experiences we have as a youth minister. Do we let them dominate? How do we sound when we talk about our ministry? What comes through in our conversations? Is it our excitement or frustration, our joys or problems? Are we more positive or negative about our ministry? We need to articulate that this is an exciting and challenging ministry. These are wonderful young people searching for a sense of God and in need of a faith community.

Finally, how do we act or look? We all know that working with young people requires a particular ability to relate to them. But we also know that this does not mean we have to look like, sound like, and act like teenagers. Distancing ourselves from young people in the way we look and behave and yet remaining close to them is not easy and takes determination.

> Since adolescence seems to extend into the mid-twenties [for many people], one might wonder how effectively one can distance oneself from teenagers. Well, it was tough [for me].

However, it is very necessary to be able to do so in ministry. Objectivity is essential for true adult advocacy for youth. Though our ministry is to and with young people, we don't abdicate being adults or professional. Just as we model what it means to be a believing, Christian adult for young people, we should also model what it means to be a professional, adult youth minister. One youth minister in my survey suggested that we "be confident, but not coolly." We also need to model to other adults what it means to be mature and professional, especially in our official interactions with them as members of parish staffs, civic organizations, or the like.

Inadequate salaries and benefits: Perhaps you have seen the bumper sticker about being Christian that says The Pay Is Not Much, But the Benefits Are Out of This World. This may be true, but laboring for minimal salary because ministry is the work of the Lord also reflects the myth The church owns my soul, and often becomes a factor in our longevity in youth ministry.

Though we seldom enter youth ministry for the money, determining an appropriate and just salary right at the beginning is an important survival strategy. In doing so, several things should be considered: the education, training, and experience of the minister; the major areas of responsibility; the size and complexity of the program; the amount of program administration; and the volunteer management and supervision responsibilities. Compensation policies and guidelines may vary from parish to parish and from diocese to diocese. However, a standard package includes salary, health insurance, pension, appropriate liability insurance, professional development assistance, annual leave policy, sick days allowance, and car use allowance.

Even before you are hired, hold out for a parish which will also meet some of your needs: professional needs, pastoral needs, the need for true support. Don't feel you have to take the first offer that comes to you! Interview the parish as much as the pastor or search committee interviews you. Accept rejection, but more importantly, learn to dish it out. Accepting less-than-adequate (or grossly unfair) terms or conditions of contract only perpetuates the dysfunctional systems that offer them and the dysfunctional managerial styles that support them.

> People should not be afraid to insist that a salary offer is too low. The more this is done, the more reality will slap the church in the face. Also, we have collections for the education of our seminarians (many of whom bug out!)—why not begin to insist that the same level of financial commitment go to the laity (the true backbone of our church)?

Obviously, the issue of compensation can be very emotional and a major source of frustration for those in full-time, professional ministry. The church needs to continue its commitment to providing just and fair compensation for all its ministers and not settling for the merely minimal.

The task of identifying the sources of tension, conflict, and frustration in our ministry is critical. Only when we have done so can we take a proactive approach to dealing with them. Only then can we make decisions about possible changes in our work styles, behaviors, perceptions, or situations that will enable ministry to be a rewarding and growthful experience.

Reflection: Facing Your Longevity Factors

① Which of the following factors have the greatest positive effect on your longevity in youth ministry? the greatest negative effect?

adult team	parents	resources
expectations	staff	youth
funding	vision	pastor

② For a full day, listen to your language and your tone of
    voice as you talk about your ministry, the young people,
    and your setting (parish, school, diocese, etc.). How often
    do you hear negative or pessimistic phrases of speech or
    tones of voice?

③ Think about the tensions and frustrations in your ministry.

    a. What are the major sources of tension and frustration?

    b. What was the most critical tension or frustration in
       your first year of youth ministry? How has it changed?
       Has it lessened? increased?

    c. What is the most critical tension or frustration you
       have right now? How might you be contributing to it?
       How might it be resolved?

④ Recall a recent conflict you had in any area of your min-
    istry.

    a. What was the cause of this conflict?

    b. How did you handle this conflict?

    c. What was the outcome of this conflict?

    d. Looking back, what would have been helpful in this
       conflict?

⑤ Consider the support you experience in your ministry.

    a. On a scale of 1 (low) to 10 (high), what level of sup-
       port do you experience? Explain.

    b. From whom do you receive most of your support?

    c. From whom do you need more support?

The Cost of Excellence

Excellence: the state or art of excelling; the condition of surpassing or outdoing. Doesn't this sound just like youth ministry! We do strive to be excellent, to offer the best and most comprehensive ministry we can. Since many of us approach youth ministry with this frame of mind, it is a good strategy to take a look at our job from the viewpoint of striving for excellence. We need to recognize the costs as well as the rewards of doing youth ministry with this perspective.

Personally, the costs might include putting in extra hours of work, giving up much of our personal time, never having a free weekend, feeling isolated from friends and family, and feeling anxiety and stress—all of which can degenerate physical, emotional, and spiritual health.

However, striving for excellence also yields payoffs. We might enhance our self-esteem, confidence, self-satisfaction, and reputation. We learn to risk new ventures, trust our judgment, and receive recognition for our accomplishments.

Five Great Proverbs

Here are five great proverbs to keep in mind when striving for excellence in youth ministry:
▶ We can be victims of our own theology of ministry.
▶ We can be victims of our own professionalism.
▶ Reality doesn't change, only our perception of reality can change.
▶ We have to maintain a broad perspective.
▶ Being excellent is better than being mediocre.
Each of these proverbs can influence the decisions we make about our use of time, energy, and talents, and, consequently, affect our ability to balance the personal, family, relational, spiritual, and ministerial aspects of our life.

37

We can be victims of our own theology of ministry. Len Sperry, MD, PhD, in his article "Determinants of a Minister's Well-Being," identifies two widely differing theologies of ministry.[1] In one theology, the call to ministry is heard as a call to personal responsibility in accomplishing the mission that the ministry serves. The focus of our time and talent is on accomplishing the mission. If ministry is service and we are ministers, then our life is totally committed to carrying out service. In this theology, much importance is placed on creating and upholding the structures and systems that enable the ministry to happen efficiently. Establishing policies, recognizing authority, and maintaining hierarchical and firm control are given a high priority. This understanding of ministry focuses on action, results, and doing, and the health and well-being of the minister usually comes in second to accomplishing the mission.

Most of us have worked with ministers who operate from this understanding. We ourselves may have articulated this theology as we tried to explain why we didn't have time for fun, relationships, family, or even prayer.

In the other theology, ministry is understood as a commitment to maintaining the Lord's wholeness in ministry. This theology sees Jesus as one who serves others through healing, caring, compassion, and teaching. But it also sees him as one who took time away in the mountains to pray, to be with friends, to cultivate relationships, and to stay in close touch with God. This is a much more holistic and complete understanding of the ministry to which that Jesus calls us.

In this theology, doing springs from being, action from contemplation. Ministry is characterized by presence, mutuality, empowerment, and transformation. Lifestyle blends loving service to others with loving concern for self . . . without guilt.

We can be victims of our own professionalism. As persons advocating for professionalism in youth ministry, we must be careful about how professionalism is defined. We need to distinguish between professionalism and perfectionism. Professionalism requires a level of competence in the ministry as well as involves responsibility for significant, if not all, aspects of the youth ministry program.

Perfectionism is very different. According to Len Sperry, perfectionists tend to believe in the obligation of the three Os: "omnipotence, omniscience, and omnipresence" (p. 22).

Omnipotence means that the minister must take responsibility for everything, making it very difficult to delegate decision making to others. This is also a mark of the Lone Ranger minister, one who is unable to let go of any aspects of the program.

Omniscience suggests that the minister should know and be able to do everything in her or his work. The omniscience trap can be sprung from the side of the youth minister who believes that she or he has to be totally competent in everything, or from the side of the faith community or staff who believe that the youth minister should be the ultimate expert in everything.

Omnipresence portrays the minister as available to serve twenty-four hours a day, seven days a week, precluding any time for rest, recreation, and any other healthy activity.

Sperry states that individuals who consciously or unconsciously live by the obligations of the three Os often exhibit "anxiety, depression, guilt, self-doubt, and chronic frustration" (p. 22).

These three Os do not serve as appropriate characteristics of professionalism and, moreso, will severely hinder our longevity in youth ministry. Defining professionalism in terms of omnipotence, omniscience, and omnipresence sets up an impossible dichotomy between being professional and being healthy.

Sociologist Joseph Fichter, SJ, at the request of the U.S. Catholic Conference of Bishops, studied the health of the clergy across the United States. His findings about the clergy are very applicable to those in youth ministry. Fichter discovered five basic health behaviors that contribute to staying physically fit: "maintaining sensible weight, getting enough sleep, getting sufficient exercise, not smoking, and moderating alcohol intake" (p. 22). Wouldn't this list make for interesting discussion with a group of people involved in youth ministry!

Fichter's study also found "a high correlation between physical health and psychological health" (p. 22). Those who noted that they were in good physical health were also likely to report good emotional and mental balance.

Researchers note that ministers prone to chronic stress tend to share a number of psychological characteristics. These include idealism and overcommitment, a high drive for achievement, a high need for approval from others, vulnerability to the excessive demands of others, guilt about meeting one's own needs, a sense of hurry and impatience, and perfectionism. These characteristics are pretty common for people in youth ministry.

Given the crucial relationships between physical, emotional, relational, and spiritual health, a complete definition of professionalism will also include the importance of good friendships, family relationships, recreation and play, a regular prayer life, a healthy sense of self, and realistic goals. We need to balance time spent with others, time spent for others, and time spent with and for ourselves.

Reality doesn't change, only our perception of reality can change. In some real sense, we create our own heaven . . . and hell. The lens through which we perceive our ministry situation, the young people with whom we minister, and our role in our work critically alters our judgments, feelings, and attitudes. The effect here is similar to seeing the glass half-empty or half-full. The reality is the same in either case, but the perception of the viewer can be very different. As discussed in chapter 2, our perceptions are greatly influenced by any underlying myth we might hold about church and ministry. However, we have the power to identify such myths, and therefore we can evaluate the accuracy of our perceptions.

Perceived reality is the reality we deal with. Our actions, decisions, and emotions are influenced by the world as we understand it to be. Our perceptions become our maps and paradigms. What happens when our observations are not an accurate depiction of reality? We get confused and lost. What happens when the way we see a situation is different from the real situation? We act on faulty information. Whether it be a pastor who seems to dislike young people or a school principal who resists allowing teenagers to use the gym after school, we will handle a situation as we perceive it to be. We can't change the reality, but we can change our perceptions of it.

Three positive assumptions might influence our perception of people and situations:

▶ We can assume that people are generally of good will. Most people are good; the inherently bad or evil person is rare. Even the least comfortable or most difficult people we encounter in our ministry are good people. They, too, are made in the image and likeness of God.

▶ We can assume that people are generally well intentioned. Most people are trying hard to live out a vision of life or church or ministry that seems authentic to them. Most people really want to do what's best, even those with whom we have the greatest difficulty.

▶ We can assume that people are unique. We all have different values, different motives, and different needs. Personality inventories like the Myers-Briggs, the Keirsey Bates Temperament Sorter, and the Enneagram point out that we think differently, understand differently, and act differently. We have different goals and want different things from our ministry. And that's OK! It really is OK to be different, and it is a self-sprung trap to expect others to be exactly like us, regardless of how "normal" we may perceive ourselves to be.

If we knew enough of each person's story, we'd find that most people have understandable reasons for acting the way they do. Most of us have experienced meeting the parents of a young person in our program and thinking to ourselves, for better or for worse, "So, that's why he (or she) acts that way." Knowing someone and their situation makes it easier to understand their behavior, even if we don't like or accept that behavior. Since we'll probably never know the history of most of the people with whom we have contact, especially the difficult people, we have to make a proactive choice to work for understanding. We can't change the reality of a person, so our only recourse is to change our perception—attitude, behavior, approach—in order to deal with him or her more effectively. We can choose to believe that even difficult people are good and well meaning, and try to work with them—or we can choose to be frustrated or angry, and work against them.

Our skills and competence also play a major part in the way we perceive people or situations. Abraham Maslow said that if the only tool we have is a hammer, we tend to see every problem as a nail. If we have developed a variety of skills for dealing with people, every problem or problem person doesn't have to be seen as a nail. The more we have developed our skills and competence for dealing with different situations, the more probable will be the accuracy of our perceptions of their reality, and the more we will feel capable of handling them. When this is the case, we're not so apt to overreact, feel trapped, or get depressed. For example, if we have developed conflict management or assertiveness skills, we can more easily and calmly choose to confront a conflict with a co-worker. Or if we have developed the skills of a change agent, we will see more opportunities for building a comprehensive youth ministry in a place that hasn't previously done much along these lines.

Monitoring our perceptions is an important part in a healthy striving for excellence. Seeing realities for what they actually are makes it possible for us to alter our lifestyle if it's *really* become unhealthy and out of balance, makes it possible to cancel a youth ministry activity if there *really* isn't enough support or assistance, makes it possible to take some time off when we *really* need it—makes it more possible to survive in youth ministry.

We have to maintain a broad perspective. To direct our attitudes and behavior in ways that are healthy, we need to maintain a broad perspective of our life and in our ministry. Being able to see our situation as part of the bigger picture will help us strive for excellence. We need to consider honestly the importance of the issues that immediately confront us, in the light of even bigger and more long-range issues. A youth minister gave me a sweatshirt with the saying Compared to Nuclear War, This Is No Big Deal! This suggests one way of keeping a wholesome perspective: ask yourself, Compared with nuclear war, just how important is this issue? How much physical and emotional energy should I be investing in it?

Certainly, there are issues that are integral to professional youth ministry—issues that are worth our investment of time and energy. For example, developing an effective, comprehensive youth ministry is an issue if the parish refuses or is unable to provide space, materials, and the services of interested adults. Likewise, trying to move beyond a classroom model for adolescent catechesis becomes an important issue if the director of religious education, pastor, or parents don't understand the principles or methodology outlined in *The Challenge of Adolescent Catechesis: Maturing in Faith* document from the NFCYM.[2] These are difficult situations, and remain so even when we maintain a broad perspective. But even in these situations the bigger picture can be a help in devising strategies for dealing with important issues.

On the other hand, a pastor who doesn't get involved with the teenagers or a principal who doesn't seem very supportive of youth ministry efforts in the school or parish might not be a major issue. Of course, their involvement would be an excellent sign value to the teens. But perhaps they are very busy with their ministry, or they really trust us to direct the youth programs, or they aren't really comfortable around young people (in which case, it's better for them to stay clear). As long as we have authorization to do the ministry, we can count our blessings and get on with our program. It's a question of keeping a broad perspective.

The Serenity Prayer may have been written for us: "Lord, grant me the courage to change the things I can, the patience to accept the things I can't, and the wisdom to know the difference."

Another aspect of the challenge to keep a broad perspective involves us personally. Remember that this ministry has the potential to become all-consuming, completely taking over our personal, relational, and family life. We need to ask ourselves the questions: Five years from now, what do we want our memories of this ministry to be? What do we want to look back on? We are always creating memories, consciously and unconsciously, and if we seriously consider what we want our memories of this experience to be, we may be able to better maintain perspective in our work. Do we only want memories of twenty-four-hour days, frustration at working without support, and feeling overwhelmed? Or do we want memories of using our gifts effectively, investing our time and energy wisely, and feeling that we've received as much as we've given? Looking ahead to future memories is a way of setting priorities for efforts and making decisions about lifestyle. Perhaps we can make certain changes now to begin providing better balance in lifestyle and a more effective approach to youth ministry.

The perspective adage on my sweatshirt may also hold for deciding what to do about situations that seem insufferable. Perhaps, compared with nuclear war, leaving this job or this volunteer position is no big deal. And it might be the healthiest and wisest decision at this time. More on this is coming in chapter 5.

Being excellent is better than being mediocre. In spite of all the cautioning about striving for excellence, most of us still want to be excellent. Our theology of ministry, our definition of professionalism, our perception of the real situation of young people in the church and in society today, and our perspectives on ministry all move us to do the best job possible. We want to provide the most effective and comprehensive ministry to young people that is allowed by our skills and the parish's, school's, or community's resources. Striving for excellence is understandable and laudable, as long as we survive to enjoy it!

Reflection: Counting the Costs of Excellence

① The five great proverbs listed on page 37 affect all of us and our ministry in some fashion, and sometimes in combination.

  a. Which of the great proverbs most strikes home for you?

  b. How have any of the proverbs affected your approach to ministry?

② Maintaining good health behaviors is critical to surviving in youth ministry.

  a. On a scale of 1 (unhealthy) to 5 (healthy), how do you rate yourself in the following behaviors?

    maintaining a sensible weight _____
    getting enough sleep _____
    getting sufficient exercise _____
    not smoking _____
    moderating your alcohol intake _____

  b. In terms of your physical health, what is your strong point?

  c. In terms of your physical health, what is your weak point?

  d. Jot down on a separate sheet of paper all the activities or behaviors that would help you keep in good physical shape, that would fit into your lifestyle, and that you would enjoy doing.

  e. Select one of the activities or behaviors that would contribute to your physical health and describe the positive benefits from it.

  f. Decide when you will do this activity or begin this behavior. Be practical: determine when, where, and with whom (if appropriate). At the end of two weeks, evaluate your decision and commitment. Did you really make physical health a priority? Or did you fail to fulfill your commitment?

  g. On a separate piece of paper, make a list of healthy activities in the mental, relational, and spiritual realms. Select one activity or behavior in each realm, implement it, and evaluate it at the end of two weeks.

③ It is good for us to examine our theology of ministry and our understanding of professionalism, because they greatly affect our experience of working in youth ministry.

   a. To which theology of ministry do you personally subscribe? Which is actually reflected in your approach to youth ministry? Are they the same, or different? What are the implications of this?

   b. Omnipotence . . . omniscience . . . omnipresence: which of these three obligations do you tend toward most? What would happen if you dropped this obligation?

   c. Do you need to change your perception of any area of your ministry in order to be more healthy? What change do you need to make? What would be the benefits if you could make this change?

   d. Have you lost perspective in any area of your ministry? What has been the effect on you? How can you regain a healthy perspective?

④ *Excellence:* the state or art of excelling; the condition of surpassing or outdoing.

   a. What is the cost of the pursuit of excellence, for you personally? for your parish's (or school's, etc.) ministry?

   b. What are the rewards of excellence, for you personally? for your parish's (or school's , etc.) ministry?

   c. What are the implications of these costs and rewards of excellence?

Practical Strategies for Survival

Ten Basic Survival Strategies

Ten basic, overriding strategies are essential for survival in youth ministry. These strategies are not primarily aimed at making our ministry more effective. They are, first of all, means for helping us survive as more balanced and healthy persons, which, in turn, will make us more effective as ministers.

Be an advocate for your vision . . . and your job. Whether volunteer or salaried staff, youth ministers must be the first advocates for their vision of youth ministry, as well as for their position.

Most people in our faith communities are not familiar with a comprehensive vision of youth ministry. Many remember back

> [My concern is] coping with the frustration that youth ministry is often not seen as a profession. There is an attitude of "anyone can do it." I guess my major concern which sums up all of this is how to cope with the frustration of not being taken seriously either as a professional or as a minister, as well as having the program seen as a "token" something for the young people.

to their own teen years and their experience of the church's ministry to youth, which was usually CCD, social groups, or athletic groups, and that has become their criteria for evaluating the ministry today.

We need to raise the community's consciousness of current approaches and understanding of youth ministry. We can accomplish this in several nonimposing ways:

▶ Use the parish bulletin (or its equivalent) to publicize what is happening and what has happened in the youth ministry program. The bulletin is rarely effective for reaching young people, but it is a prime means to educate adults. A good rule of thumb is to have in the bulletin every week something about the young people in your community and about the youth ministry program.

▶ Have a youth ministry bulletin board in a conspicuous place in the parish. This will reach young people, but it also educates the adults.

▶ Use a calendar board on the wall in your office—if you have one!—or youth meeting space. List all the meetings, and evening and weekend activities. This lets people who come into your office know that youth ministry is hardly ever a nine-to-five job.

▶ Present written monthly reports at parish staff or council meetings, describing the activities, number of participating young people and adults, individual contacts with young people (the core of the ministry, but difficult to record), meetings, and important issues. If you don't attend staff or council meetings, or if they aren't regularly held, send the reports to all members of the parish staff or council.

▶ Use time sheets, if required by your parish, school, or organization, to demonstrate where your time is spent.

▶ Use your youth ministry budget to educate the community. Instead of requesting a bottom-line amount, list and describe the various activities and expenses by the components of youth ministry or some other schema that effectively outlines comprehensive youth ministry. (See *A Vision of Youth Ministry* for a discussion of youth ministry components.)[1]

▶ Be visible to the faith community, to the youth, and to the youth's parents. Attend parish events, go to a different eucharistic celebration each weekend, and attend appropriate parish meetings.

▶ Establish professional ties both within the parish (through staff meetings, informal meetings, various committees) and outside the parish (through professional gatherings of youth ministers). As important as programming and youth are, equally important is the recognition of youth ministry as a professional and necessary entity in the church community.

▶ Provide opportunities for the significant people in the community to meet your young people. Invite the pastor, principal, parish staff, parish council president, and others to come to a youth activity and introduce them to the young people. Also, offer to have a young person, or a youth panel, address the parish council or a parents group about teen issues in their relationship with church, with their parents, or with one another.

▶ Find ways to share your vision and how it relates to and benefits the faith community. Speak at the eucharistic celebration on World Day of Youth Sunday. Write letters to parents about the parish program, their practical involvement, and their youth. Post articles on youth ministry and youth concerns on bulletin boards.

> I got to know the people of the parish community, not just the teenagers, but the community as a whole. This was important because each community is unique and if you don't understand the people, it is difficult to minister to the young people in [the community].

Develop working relationships with the staff. Not only can the parish staff be a source of professional and personal support, but often they are the ones who know how the parish system works and who the major players are.

> [I made a mistake in] not establishing close ties with the faculty and staff of the school.

> I sat down with a group of young people from the parish to discuss their needs and goals. I established firm and lasting relationships with the core group of youth in the parish.

Get to know the parish or school secretary. This person usually knows the most about the organization and its operation. Offer to do in-service training for the staff or faculty on youth issues. Offer workshops for the parents of the youth.

> [It's important to] get to know your parish. The people, all the people, are so important for the support of the program. Don't alienate parents by making it seem like you have all the knowledge and therefore becoming more important than they are in their teenagers' life.

If you are new to a youth ministry position, you have about six months to ask all the important questions. Half a year is the difference between innocence and incompetence, between being new and being stupid. Use your initial innocence to your advantage for both meeting other staff and getting information. Ask questions: "Where do young people meet here?" "How do we gather our young people in our parish?" "What is the community's vision of youth ministry?" "How do we get the keys for the rooms or building?" "How do we handle printing?"

A critical task is building a working relationship with the pastor. The pastor often serves as your supervisor, evaluator, and primary source of support. Here are some practical keys to developing an effective working relationship with the pastor:

▶ Minimize surprises. Tell the pastor about any problems—teens drinking on retreat, a broken window or wall, and the like—and do so before a parent or someone else does.
▶ Communicate. Inform the pastor of your plans, either at staff meetings or in writing.

> At first, I emphasized building relationships with the staff . . . and worked closely with the department of religious education.

▶ Ask good questions and ask for advice. This enables the pastor to feel some ownership in the youth ministry program. But don't overdo it, for then it looks like incompetence.
▶ Support the pastor. Be supportive of the pastor's ministry and leadership. Don't complain about the pastor behind the pastor's back, especially to parishioners. Sharing any frustrations with the pastor in a support group is one thing, but it's quite another to complain about the pastor publicly.
▶ Recognize that the pastor is the boss. Pastoral management is the pastor's ministry, and you are part of the team. You may have to adjust to the pastor's particular management style.
▶ Find out the pastor's vision. You have to work within this vision for the parish. Try to situate the vision of youth ministry within it.
▶ Involve the pastor in the youth program on the level at which the pastor is interested and comfortable. Enable the pastor to be with young people in some way.

Maintain a healthy balance in the use of your time. Remember that a boat needs both a sail and a keel in order to keep upright and on course. Our friends, family, and outside interests are our keel, providing stability in our life. Our ministry is our sail, moving with the Spirit and the energy of our young people. A keel is not usually in sight like a sail, so we need be alert to it and to tend to it by committing the time to be with good people and to do things on our personal want-to-do list.

> [My mistake at the beginning was] not having a day off scheduled, and not giving myself enough personal time away from the church.

We should plan to take one or two days off each week—and honor that time off; it's not to be used for planning youth ministry—and two or three evenings off each week. These are averages. In youth ministry, we encounter natural crunch times when we do need to put in longer hours and more days. But by keeping time sheets or a good calendar, we can take more time off during a slower period of the ministry year.

> Have that sacred day off and do not fill it up with any church work. Watch how much you work. Be aware of the super-youth minister syndrome that is so easy to get into but so difficult to back out of.

Remember that it is unhealthy not to take time off. Working without a break can be a symptom of a need to be needed, and it fosters overachieving and burnout. It is important to ask, "Do I control my ministry, or does it control me?"

When we are new to youth ministry, we are easily caught in the trap of initial excitement and zeal. We want to do it all, and we want to do it by next week! This attitude neglects personal needs and creates a dangerous work style that may be difficult to alter at a later point—like when we get frustrated or overwhelmed.

An effective way to monitor work habits is to keep a journal or diary. Make daily entries that list hours worked, tasks, frustrations, and important insights. Keep it brief, and read it monthly.

Be in touch with your own gifts. Simply knowing who you are, complete with your strengths and weaknesses, your gifts and needs, will help you survive in this ministry. Be patient with yourself and take the time to settle into the position. Don't try to model yourself on some other great youth minister. One youth minister in my survey said, "I got a bit peeved at the constant mention of how wonderful my predecessor was!" This type of unfair comparison is an especially insidious source of frustration. Remember, your situation, your resources, and the young people you work with are different from any other's.

When starting out in a position, ask yourself, What did I inherit? Who did I inherit? This assessment will help you identify how to use your strengths and talents in developing the program, as well as how to avoid some pitfalls.

> [It's very important] to help others see the need for their help in the program. Just because you are hired on does not mean you are suppose to do it all. It's important to learn how to delegate.

On the other hand, respect what is already in place and how things normally happen. Don't try to change what needs changing all at once. People resist change, even change for the good. So plan the necessary changes in a strategic manner and create ownership for them by involving, in the planning and implementation process, the people they will most directly affect.

Develop an adult team. Recall that the Lone Ranger approach is not appropriate for youth ministry. Even in Exodus we find Jethro saying to Moses, whom he sees trying to handle all disputes by himself: "'What you are doing is not good. You will surely wear yourself out, both you and these people with you. For the task is too heavy for you; you cannot do it alone'" (Exod. 18:17–18). Being the Lone Ranger also reflects a poor understanding of ministry. We are called to be enablers of ministry, not the doers of all ministry. So we are challenged to identify and call forth the gifts others might have for ministry.

Developing an adult team fosters the sense that it's "the parish's ministry" and not "your ministry." Teams provide a greater range of expertise and resources for a comprehensive program. More can be done for young people if more adults are available to minister.

You will need four key ingredients to form an effective adult team:

▶ Develop a clear mission statement for your community's youth ministry.
▶ Integrate time for prayer, sharing, and support into all team meetings.

▶ Develop for the team a job description that includes when the team will meet and that defines the team's purpose.

▶ Develop job descriptions for particular leadership roles on the adult team, such as coordinator, secretary-treasurer, sports coordinator, activities coordinator, publicity coordinator, and so forth. Include role responsibilities, necessary qualifications, and required time commitment. If possible, ask the adult team members themselves to help develop these job descriptions.

The team could also develop descriptions for the other jobs to be done in the program, such as those of retreat coordinator, catechist, service coordinator, and chaperon. Having specific job descriptions will make it easier to recruit volunteers for your program. People are more likely to commit to a definite job that has clear responsibilities and a specified time period.

Develop a support group. A support group is different from the adult team. The adult team benefits the work of the ministry, whereas the support group benefits you. Two basic kinds of support groups exist. One kind is composed of youth ministry peers who gather on a regular basis for prayer, sharing, networking, and professional development. This kind of support group can function in various ways—for example, in all-day sessions, breakfast clubs, or dinner meetings.

Another kind of support group includes people who are not ministry staff or volunteers. We also need to interact with friends and acquaintances outside the ministerial world. If this doesn't happen routinely and regularly, we may need to form a support group of this kind to help provide a more balanced perspective on life, personal concerns, and "real" issues. Sometimes we just need to have conversations about concerns and topics other than young people, youth ministry, or church.

It's important to know where your support is, not just within the parish, but outside. Who are the other folks experiencing the same thing—those experiencing the need for youth ministry bonding? (A key concern) is networking so youth ministers can support each other.

> I found it important to have a support system
> of family, friends, and fellow professionals for
> feedback and sharing. This helped me maintain
> perspective.

For developing either kind of support group, follow these steps:

1. Admit you need a support group.
2. Take the initiative. Use your diocesan youth ministry office (or its equivalent) to begin networking, or simply gather interested people in your area. Discuss people's expectations and needs and set some parameters for how the group will meet, who will lead prayer, how food and refreshments will be handled.
3. Schedule support time. Put it on the calendar and honor the commitment. Schedule prayer and recreation into the gatherings.
4. Be patient. Developing a support group takes time, but the payoffs are worth the investment.

Set realistic goals. Whether you are starting from scratch with a brand-new program or revamping an existing program, three years are usually needed to establish an effective youth ministry. The first year is spent setting direction, trying activities, and building awareness among the young people and the faith community. The second year is a period for looking back and evaluating the previous year, trying new approaches, experimenting with various planning and leadership models, and beginning to expand the range of ministry. In the third year, the structures for supporting comprehensive youth ministry can finally be put in place. By this time, a certain consciousness or awareness is hopefully established in the faith community. Youth ministry is no longer the "new" ministry in the parish; it has some history and tradition. Youth ministry now belongs.

For a new person, to give oneself that three years is a good strategy. One youth minister in the survey said, "When I first started in church youth ministry, I made goals to cover the first three years or so." Don't try to do everything in the first year. Not only will that overburden you, but too much too soon will also overwhelm the young people. Initially, plan for graduated successes—singles, not home runs! Do a few thing well. Developing a track record of effective and enjoyable events will build the youth's interest and establish your credibility in the community.

> Persuade the parish council to commit to long-range planning at a general parish level and institute this practice in your own ministry as well. Keep goals and objectives reasonable and maintain flexibility. It is much easier to track successes and shortcomings when this type of built-in system of evaluation and accountability is in place.

In your planning, watch for the "numbers trap." We often plan for quality and evaluate on quantity. Give quality at least as much weight in evaluating the program as you do quantity. Offering quality experiences for a small number of young people is OK. Actually, quantity will follow upon quality. Getting the word to spread among the young people that youth activities are not boring (the ultimate criticism) will take time, but is the most effective promotion of the program.

However, the numbers can be used for evaluation. If no one is participating in the youth ministry program, then perhaps you are doing the wrong kind of activities or offering them at the wrong time. An effective needs assessment should identify the activities that are most appealing to your young people, as well as the best time—day and hour—for gathering young people in your parish. When my home parish started a youth ministry program, the team assumed that Sunday evening was the best time for gathering young people. After all, most of the surrounding parishes held their programs on Sunday evenings and Sundays were more convenient for the adults. At the end of the first year, we did a needs assessment and found that our young people preferred Monday evenings because of family commitments and homework on Sundays. The youth also said that having our gatherings on Monday would help break up the school week. The team instituted the change, and the numbers of young people increased steadily, eventually doubling.

Keeping perspective when setting goals and objectives for the program keeps those goals and objectives realistic and establishes realistic criteria for success.

> I didn't handle the small turnout well, but I didn't know how to get the youth to come.
>
> Have patience! Not everything will draw the numbers, but if you are committed to the program and have youth feel an ownership in the program, then success will slowly follow.

Develop the skills that count. Competence is a major aspect of professionalism. Therefore, it is reasonable that we develop the skills necessary for effective youth ministry. Most dioceses offer training in the vision, methodology, and components of youth ministry. Youth ministers are increasingly aware of the current emphases in youth ministry, such as integrating a family perspective, including a social justice component, infusing the multicultural dimension, fostering a comprehensive pastoral care of our young people, developing an effective catechetical component, and enhancing our approaches to outreach and evangelization.

Along with competencies in those broad areas are competencies that are specific to the work of coordinating youth ministry efforts, such as the following:

▶ program development (planning, implementation, and evaluation)
▶ time and stress management
▶ delegation and enablement
▶ problem solving, decision making, and conflict management
▶ volunteer management (recruiting, training, supporting, and evaluating volunteers)
▶ administration and budgeting

Developing good skills will enable us to take better care of ourselves. One youth minister in the survey found himself "getting into counseling situations and not knowing when to get someone else involved or when to refer [to other professional services]." Another youth minister in the survey identified the first step in increasing competency as "learning who my resources were both in the parish and in the diocese and using them." This minister added, "I also attended workshops to get a better grasp of what I was doing." We need to be proactive about identifying the skills our positions require and securing the necessary training.

Shake the dust from your sandals. Youth ministry is a legitimate, lifelong vocation and career . . . but not for everyone. Some of us may have to confront the reality that we may be called to a different ministry where our gifts are more appropriate. The decision either to leave ministry altogether or to change ministerial roles is very difficult and requires honest soul-searching. A process of prayer and discernment is helpful in coming to the best—the healthiest—decision.

When the prompting for a move seems to be coming from inside ourselves, a simple criteria for staying or going is to look at what the fruits of the labor are for ourselves:

▶ Am I growing personally, ministerially, and spiritually in this position?
▶ Am I happy in this role?
▶ Am I doing good work in this role?

If the answer to one or more of these questions is no, then perhaps other options have to be considered. However, we may find that even when the program is going very well, we are growing, and we are doing good work, we still feel a need to move on to something else. We may intuitively know that we have stayed too long in this ministry. We may find that we are looking for excuses to stay even while something inside is telling us it's time to go.

Sometimes, the external setting may be the primary prompter for making a move. Despite our best efforts and skills and the good intentions of the parish or school, things don't always work out. Sometimes the mix of the individual and the setting just isn't right. In this case, several considerations may help us decide whether to move on to a new setting or to leave the ministry:

▶ Ask: Am I running away, or running toward something? Am I motivated by my fears or by my dreams?
▶ Ask: Am I seeing things clearly and realistically? Am I being honest with myself? Am I blaming "them," making the situation someone else's fault or responsibility? Is my perception of this reality an accurate one?

▶ Be open with your struggle. Find an objective person who knows you and the situation and is willing to give you honest feedback on your perceptions, insights, and concerns.

▶ Remember the Serenity Prayer: "Lord, grant me the courage to change the things I can, the patience to accept the things I can't, and the wisdom to know the difference."

▶ Remind yourself that quitting is not failure and that leaving a ministry position does not make you a bad person.

▶ Feel God's presence in all of this. No door closes without a window opening. Practice discernment in your decision making. Bring your faith and trust in God's loving providence into the process.

If the parish or school is really not invested in or committed to youth ministry, then let it go . . . move on. You can only really change yourself, not the parish or the school. Regardless of your level of concern and your investment of energy, you may not be able to change the situation.

These considerations will likely hold true when the leaving or moving on is not our choice. Even when we are released from a ministry position, we have to honestly assess the situation and our part in the problem. The German philosopher Goethe said, That which does not kill me, makes me stronger. Out of the pain and uncertainty of leaving a ministry position comes the possibility of new opportunities and personal growth.

Take care of your relationship with God. Does my spirituality flow from my ministry, or does my ministry flow from my spirituality? This is the classic chicken-and-the-egg dilemma. But it is best not to worry about which comes first. A both-and approach is the best one. Our work should nourish our relationship with God, and our relationship with God should feed our ministry. As one youth minister in the survey put it, "Give as much time and energy to your prayer life as anything else—otherwise, it seems like a lot of trouble for nothing." Strategies for caring for our spirituality are treated in chapter 6.

Reflection: Applying Basic Survival Strategies

① We must identify and strengthen the basic, overriding strategies that enable us to survive this ministry and to maintain our emotional, physical, and spiritual balance.

　　a. What is one of the techniques you use to maintain balance in your ministry?

　　b. Of the strategies identified in this chapter, which one do you need to implement immediately?

　　c. What ministry skill would enhance your survival, if you were to develop it more fully?

② Delegation is more than simply giving away our responsibilities and tasks. It really empowers people to use their gifts for the good of the community.

　　a. Jot down on a separate sheet of paper the tasks or responsibilities that you could reasonably delegate, and the people who could currently fulfill them or be trained to do so.

　　b. Choose one task or area and determine when you will contact the person who is able to fulfill it.

③ Sometimes we can more clearly see our investment in our ministry by examining what we have unknowingly given up.

　　a. Again, on a separate sheet of paper, jot down ten "delights" in your life—ten things you love to do. Next to each one, write the date of the last time you did it.

　　b. Share your list of delights with someone who knows you.

　　c. What do the dates on your list tell you about the balance in your lifestyle?

d. Next to at least five of the delights, write the next date on which you will do each.

④ We often use time charts like the one on the facing page, in leadership programs for teaching time management skills. This chart enables you to plot your work hours. On it, record the number of hours you worked for each of the past few weeks and the number you plan to work for each of the next few weeks. The left side of the chart identifies the number of hours worked each week, and the bottom of the chart identifies the weeks. Place a dot corresponding to the number of hours for each week. Then connect the dots.

  When you have completed the time chart for several weeks, answer the following questions on a separate sheet of paper:

a. Make notes explaining unusually high and low numbers—for example, identifying holidays, vacation, conferences, retreats, meetings, and the like. Using forty to forty-five hours as a "normal" week, see if the graph shows an intensive work cycle and more easily paced times.

b. What is your first reaction to the chart? Is this a "normal" time in the ministry year? How will the time chart change over the next few weeks or months?

c. Could you have had more control over the hours worked during any particular periods of time? Explain.

d. When is your intense work period? your easiest work period?

e. Can any projects or tasks be moved from the intensive work time to less intense times? Explain.

f. Do any personal obligations, responsibilities, or demands conflict with your intensive work period? Can any be moved?

g. As you review your work cycle, do you find any changes that you want to make? need to make? can make? Explain.

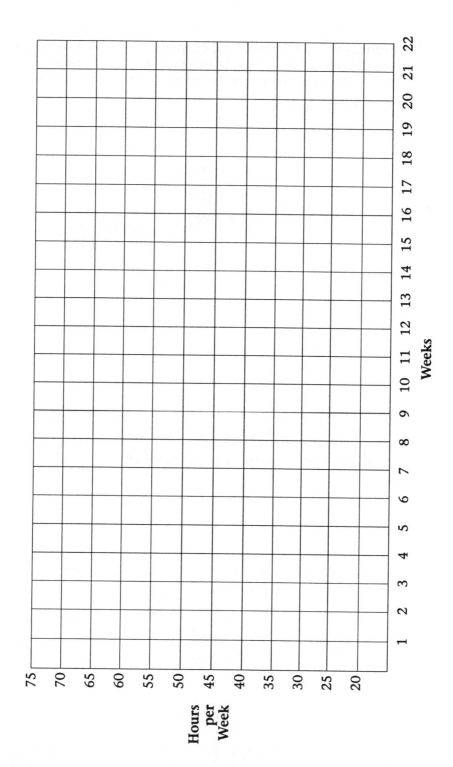

⑤ Perhaps the most difficult experience in ministry is deciding to leave or being fired from a position. If you have ever had this experience, answer the following questions:

a. What happened?

b. How did you feel at the time?

c. Where did you go for support? Did you have an objective listener?

d. In retrospect, was this a good move for you?

e. Looking back, would you like to have done anything differently? If so, what?

Spirituality

"Otherwise it seems like a lot of trouble for nothing." This statement from an experienced youth minister in the survey cap-
tures the importance of a healthy spirituality for surviving in
youth ministry. Our relationship with God, said another, is "essential to being human. It's essential to authentic ministry.
Youth sense clearly what the person who works with them is
'made of' so to speak. If fostering spirituality is a priority, it has
to be something they [youth] see as a priority for us—not in
routine practices, but as an ongoing journey." Another youth
minister in the survey wrote, "Spirituality is the seen and unseen Christ that is who we are each day, and who we are to
those with whom we are called to share life." Clearly, our spirituality is foundational to being authentic ministers with young
people as well as integral to our personal identity.

We are instinctively contemplative. We are stunned by the
beauty of life; astounded by the power of life; and overwhelmed
by the mystery in life, which is something greater, something
deeper, something more real than even what we see. The challenge is to recognize this attraction to the spiritual, to name the
obstacles that block spiritual growth, and to identify the particular strategies that foster our spirituality.

A Framework for Spirituality

A helpful framework for dealing with our spirituality is one
based on how we *see;* how we *name* what we see, and how we
act upon what we name.

How we see: Our faith has a significant effect on the way we
perceive reality. For the Christian with the eyes to see, the world
is shot through with the presence of God. We are challenged to

develop "spiritual eyes"—a spiritual sensitivity, through which we perceive every aspect of creation, every person, action, and relationship, as an opportunity to encounter the holy. Do we see ourselves as sacred—as persons created in the image and likeness of God? In meeting strangers, do we see the possibility of friendship? Do we see the poor people in our midst? And do we see the face of Jesus in poor people? Do we always see the beauty in creation, and see it as a reflection of God? Do we see our God as an intimate presence, or as a distant observer?

How we name what we see: Two people seeing the same stunning sunset may have very different experiences. For one, the sunset is a wonderful diffusion of light resulting in a beautiful display of color. For another, it is a reflection of God smiling upon the earth. The sunset is the same, but the way they name it alters the experience for them. For one, it remains just a beautiful sunset. For the other, it carries the abiding presence of God.

Another example of the effect of naming is found in how we categorize poor people. Are we saddened that they didn't make better choices in their life, or that they don't have the personal strength or perseverance to "pull themselves up" in this world? Or, in faith, do we experience poor people as a sign of the presence of Jesus pointed out by him in his words, "'Just as you did it to one of the least of these . . . , you did it to me'" (Matt. 25:40)?

Yet another example of naming is the Eucharist. Different people may attend the same liturgical ritual but name it very differently. For one person, the Eucharist is the Holy Sacrifice of the Mass. For another, the Eucharist is the commemoration of Jesus' action at the Last Supper. For still another, it is the real presence of Jesus in bread and wine. For all, it is the same ritual, but with different names and, consequently, different images having different understandings.

How we act upon what we name: The way we perceive and name our experiences, relationships, and world profoundly affects their meaning for us. And once the naming is done, we are challenged to act upon what the name communicates to us. Naming the sunset an expression of God challenges us to find expressions of God throughout all of creation. Naming Christ in poor people challenges us to act on their behalf. Naming Christ's presence in the Eucharist calls us to act upon the meaning of that presence among us.

One youth minister in my private survey of professionals saw spirituality as "the personal, daily business of recognizing [seeing] the transcendence of God in an imperfect world, of hearing God speak [naming] from within that world, and opening myself to that force or direction [acting] in my life." Another said that spirituality is "an awareness of God's presence and activity in the world and in my own life. This awareness should have a direction on how I live my life." This process of seeing, naming, and acting provides a framework for integrating the transcendent and the imminent, the sacred and the secular, the divine and the human. This framework helps define the complex nature of spirituality.

Obstacles to Spiritual Sensitivity

Here is a simple, but not simplistic, definition of spirituality: Spirituality is the quality of spirit that is present in seeing, naming, and acting upon the mystery of God's presence. To be spiritual is to see God always present to us, to name that presence as God's continuous communication to us, and to act upon that presence and that communication.

But being spiritual is not always that easy. Things get in the way. We become distracted from and even blinded to God's presence and deaf to God's communication. Therefore, we must become aware of the things that block our spiritual senses so that we can act to overcome or forestall them.

Perceived lack of time: How can we take care of our spiritual life when we're just so busy? Setting priorities for our time is difficult but crucial. We can get caught up in the ministry, responding to the needs of young people, and neglect our personal spiritual needs. Busy-ness can lead to an inability to discern God's call or God's presence. Our life can become too hectic for us to hear God's communication.

> Spirituality takes time—spirituality is a relationship and like any relationship that one wants to develop in a quality manner, a time commitment, or perhaps a priority approach, is necessary.

An unhealthy perception of being a minister: It is quite easy to tell ourselves that as a minister, we need to be always "on," to be always working. We may be reluctant to allow others to minister to us, or may even consider being ministered to as a sign that we aren't doing our job.

> Focusing too much on others at the expense of your own personal growth [is an obstacle]. The hours are so long, it is easy to be always working.

Always being on also makes it difficult to create the space necessary for a healthy prayer life. Taking time for a personal retreat experience, for example, is important to us as ministers. It's not something we save for doing when we have "free time."

Fear of change: Change is always unnerving. It is a challenge in all aspects of youth ministry and is a challenge in our spiritual life. For example, a youth minister in the survey said: "At times there may be a fear of becoming a spiritual person. What will I have to sacrifice or change? Can a spiritual person still drink beer? Will becoming more spiritual enhance my personal relationships or pull me from others?" Fear of change in spirituality often arises out of an incomplete or misguided understanding of spirituality. Depending on our understanding of spirituality, we might conclude that change is too risky and the cost too high. That is why we must think through what spirituality is, as described at the beginning of this chapter.

Lack of a support group: Just as being part of a support group enhances our effectiveness as youth ministers, belonging to a supportive faith community or participating in a faith-sharing or prayer group likewise fosters our spiritual health. We can benefit from the experiences, insights, and practices of others in this struggle to maintain an authentic spirituality.

The influence of today's media: We adults are as susceptible to the impact of media as our young people. It is easy to be influenced by the societal definitions of success, relationships, and lifestyle. We are tempted to equate self-worth with salary, possessions, and an occupation that is socially acceptable (have you ever been asked, "Do you still work with kids?"). We are all affected by societal understandings of work and leisure time. The value of a simple lifestyle is rarely portrayed in the media. And solitude, which is essential for prayer, is often deemed a waste of time.

Equating self-worth with work: In our ministry, we can begin to resemble the stereotypical "corporate person," driven to succeed at all personal costs. We define success differently, but with the same personal results. Equating our self-worth with our ministry work is a trap that can close us off from the criteria God uses to measure our worth. If we judge our effectiveness in ministry by the number of programs, meetings, and events on our calendar, we will have little chance to attend to our spiritual needs.

Dualism: Sometimes our spirituality can become separated from, rather than integrated with, our ministry. It can become compartmentalized and distinct from our ministry. This separation constitutes a dualism that prevents our spirituality and our ministry from strengthening and deepening each other. Keep in mind that our ministry should flow from our spirituality and our spirituality should be enhanced by our ministry.

Lack of a spiritual director or mentor: Because we are very involved in mentoring and directing the spiritual growth of our young people, we forget that we, too, could benefit from a spiritual mentor—one mentor that can help us develop and maintain patterns of spiritual health that can overcome or even forestall the other obstacles to our spiritual sensitivities.

Patterns of Spiritual Health

The key to overcoming or forestalling the obstacles to our spiritual sensitivities is to create patterns of spiritual health. Doris Donnelly has identified five personal patterns or characteristics that contribute to one's spiritual health.[1] Though some of these patterns or characteristics also affect other aspects of youth ministry, they are applied here specifically to the spirituality of the youth minister.

Maintains balance in life: A healthy, spiritual person knows that there is time for work, study, play, sleep, and prayer. But family, friends, leisure, and recreation also deserve our time. When balance does not exist in our life, we can fall into the trap of equating self-worth with work and blurring the line between the private elements in our life and our public ministry. If this happens, our self-identity and self-esteem are particularly vulnerable and our spiritual energy is cut off and depleted.

Cultivates important friendships: Friendships are the heart and sign of spiritual health. Friends are the people with whom we can honestly be ourselves, with our strengths and weaknesses, hopes and fears, and successes and failings. They are our primary, unofficial support group. True friends allow us to know and accept ourselves, and such authenticity is vital to our spirituality.

Deals with addictions and compulsions: In order to commit to change, we first need to name the addictions and compulsions in our life. The common addictions confronting youth ministers include drink, drugs, food, and money; the list of compulsions usually includes seeking power and control, working, doing for others, and looking for approval. These addictions and compulsions are often reinforced by the media and societal pressures.

After naming the addictions or compulsions, we have to disengage and replace them with healthy passions, including, perhaps, a passion for balance in our lifestyle.

Knows how to close gaps: A healthy spirituality causes one to accept responsibility for being an "ambassador of reconciliation." Breaks in relationships interrupt the flow of the spirit and short-circuit spirituality. We are challenged to take on Jesus' attitude of reconciliation and to bridge any gaps in our relationships and in the relationships of our family, or in the relationships of persons or groups who are hurting. We become healers in the life of those around us. We enable others to bridge the gaps in their life, while closing the gaps in our own.

Attends to God in the present moment: It is characteristic of spiritual health to be in touch with God's constant act of self-communication. God is present to us in the very ordinary experiences of our life even though we may be more aware of that presence in the extraordinary experiences.

Strategies for Fostering Spiritual Health

Several strategies will enable us to nurture the patterns of spiritual health.

Praying: Though this sounds obvious, praying may be the most difficult discipline for many of us. We have to set aside time for prayer on a daily basis. But be realistic. Begin with small steps. Set aside five or ten minutes each day to sit quietly and listen to God. Begin by listening and being aware of God's constant presence. Look ahead to the day starting to unfold, or review the day just ended. If you find that you need a guide, purchase a book of prayer that seems to fit your style. But start praying . . . today . . . now!

Using traditional spiritual practices: The traditional practices of the church offer solid ways of building up spiritual life. For example, you might fast on a regular or occasional basis—but fast for a reason, such as to be in solidarity with poor people, to confront your compulsions, or to develop personal discipline. Use other traditional spiritual practices as well—such as theological and spiritual reading; participation in the sacramental life of the faith community, including eucharistic and noneucharistic liturgies; and celebrations of the liturgical seasons, especially Advent and Lent. These traditional spiritual practices should be rediscovered, reclaimed, and investigated. They can enhance spiritual health.

Identifying holy ground: Where is your holy ground? Where can you go and know that you will encounter God? We all need our "burning bush," or need to go "back to the mountain" to encounter God. We all need our holy ground and our sacred places. Set aside the time to visit and revisit the places where you most clearly experience God's communication.

Spending time with holy people: Our holy people are those who are sacrament for us. They mediate God's presence to us. They are often those with whom we can be most intimate, most honest, and most truly ourselves. They may be our closest friends, family members, co-workers, or small children. Our holy people may also not be personally known to us. They may be those whose writing, speaking, or performing is sacrament for us, communicating God's presence to us. We need to spend time with our holy people, for they enable us to know God.

Protecting your Sabbath time: We are very good at dedicating ourselves to the work time of our ministry. However, we also need to dedicate ourselves to another kind of time: Sabbath time. (For a full development of this concept, see Tilden Edwards's *Sabbath Time*).[2]

In Genesis, we hear of God creating the world in six days (work time), but on day seven, God rests (Sabbath time). Sabbath time can be a pure resting time in the presence of God—relaxing in the love of God. It can also be active—being with friends or family, walking in the woods or along the beach. Sabbath time is a time dedicated to bringing a new experience of our connectedness to God and to God's creation—a time in which all life is seen as gifted, as an outpouring of God; a time in which we become aware of God and rest in that awareness. The need for Sabbath time underlies the commandment to keep holy the Lord's day.

Setting aside time for the desert: Jesus experienced desert times in his life—times when he needed to go up to the mountains or into the desert to renew himself. We all experience those kinds of times and need to attend to them. We need to retreat to our desert place for an extended period of renewal and refreshment.

In youth ministry language, this means that if we are to be spiritually healthy in our ministry, we must set time aside for retreat experiences, especially at desert times when we feel a real need for them. And this does not mean attending a youth retreat! Whether it be a personal, quiet experience or a meeting with other people, we must create, calendar, and then take the time for at least an annual retreat.

Finding spiritual guidance: A spiritual director or mentor can help us see our way, identify our tensions, and support us through our struggles. We need a trusted companion who walks with us on our faith journey.

We might choose as our spiritual director someone who has watched us grow and struggle in our faith throughout our life. Or perhaps we would prefer to find a person who is unfamiliar with us but who has the experiences, insight, and perspective that speak to our needs. Either way, spiritual mentors can provide us with the direction, support, and guidance we need to direct and nurture our spirituality.

One youth minister in my survey said that the key to her longevity in this work is remembering "the importance of personal prayer time and faith enrichment." Taking care of our spirituality is certainly crucial if we are to survive youth ministry. When we look to the heroes and heroines of ministry—for example, Mother Teresa, Dorothy Day, Oscar Romero, Mother Lange, and Thomas Merton (we all have our favorites)—we learn an important lesson: given the intensity of their ministries, if burnout were just a physical or emotional condition, they would have burned out early in their career. More likely, burnout is primarily a spiritual condition. When the quality of the spirit in our life suffers, we suffer and our ministry suffers. Fostering our spiritual health is a critical element in surviving youth ministry.

Reflection: Your Spiritual Well-Being

① Even those of us involved in youth ministry must take the time to diagnose our current state of spiritual well-being.

   a. How do you define spirituality?

   b. What is your spiritual temperature right now? Why?

   c. What are the obstacles that most hinder your spiritual health?

   d. What practical strategies do you follow for fostering your spiritual health?

② An important step in diagnosing our state of spiritual well-being is identifying the resources available for enhancing it.

   a. How does your ministry deepen your spirituality?

   b. How does your spirituality enhance your ministry?

   c. Who models a healthy blend of ministry and spirituality for you? Why?

   d. What is the place that most fosters your spirituality, that is your holy ground? Why?

   e. When were you last at your holy ground?

③ We must commit ourselves to taking some practical steps in order to be proactive about our spiritual health.

   a. What is one thing you can do to enhance your spiritual growth?

   b. When is the next time you will be on your holy ground?

   c. Whom would you like to ask about their "spiritual health secrets"?

Conclusion: Why Do We Stay?

Throughout this book, we have dealt primarily with the negatives of being involved in youth ministry: the tensions, the conflicts, and the frustrations. We have also examined the potential personal cost when these negative issues overwhelm us: declining physical, emotional, and spiritual health, eroded personal relationships, and even bitterness and anger toward the church.

We have identified practical strategies for overcoming these negatives and surviving, even thriving, in the ministry. Now, perhaps, the most important question remaining is, Why do we stay in this ministry? In the midst of the struggles that do arise, we must remember—or be reminded of—the benefits inherent in serving in youth ministry. What are the payoffs for us?

Payoffs in Youth Ministry

We will receive days off in purgatory? On particularly tough days, have you thought to yourself, "I'll go straight to heaven for this!"? If our God is a just God, then surely we can expect a heavenly reward for dealing with the craziness that is characteristic of youth ministry. This may not be good theology, but it certainly provides solace at times.

This ministry enhances our search for God. We are continually presented with opportunities to deepen our faith. We grow through the shared experiences of retreats, service projects, work camps, catechetical programs, and prayer with our young people. Sometimes our spiritual development is encouraged by young people ministering to us, evangelizing us, gracing us with the depths of their spirituality. And sometimes it comes through watching and listening to young people in their searching. We are indeed blessed with many opportunities to enhance our search for God.

This ministry will renew society. Our hope must be that as the younger generations come to full adulthood, the Gospel values and practices we have taught them will influence their choice of lifestyle, occupation, and vocation, and they will be happier and faith-filled persons who will make a positive difference in society.

We are responding to the Gospel. Youth ministry enables us to use our gifts and talents for building the Reign of God. We experience the excitement and the joy of responding to the Good News. Every day, we live out our baptismal commitment and the call to minister to and with the faith community.

We will be happy. Happiness is one of the basic payoffs in youth ministry. The ingredients for being happy are there. Youth ministry gives us the opportunity to do good work, to be surrounded by good people and good friends, and even to like ourselves better. We feel good because we are doing good.

This work fosters our gifts. Whatever the particular gifts are that we bring to ministry with young people, they are always being challenged or offered new opportunities to grow and expand.

This is great work. In this ministry, we are involved in the greatest mystery and power in creation. We are engaged in human life enspirited with the divine. This ministry gives us the opportunity to help young people grow physically, emotionally, relationally, and spiritually. We share in their faith journey, their relationship struggles, their questions about and hopes for the future, their concerns about local and global justice issues, their intense commitments, their pain, laughter, and joy. Few other work situations present the opportunities to touch human life the way youth ministers touch the life of young people.

Everyone likes a harvest. The scriptural image of sowing seeds is very appropriate for youth ministry. Much of our work involves sowing seeds, seeds that in many cases seem to bear little fruit. Because of the developmental character of adolescence, we may not see the fruition of our work. We are planting seeds that others may nurture, and still others may harvest. But because our God is a good God, at times we are given a harvest, are graced with the recognition or realization of the good we have done. Then we have to remember, though, that the bounty we reap started with seeds that someone else may have sown.

True ministry duplicates itself. This principle from *A Vision of Youth Ministry* reminds us of the importance of calling young people to ministry. Response to this call is also one of our rewards. We can find great satisfaction in seeing our young people, during their teen years, taking active roles in our program and in the faith community; as young adults, participating in the faith community; or as adults, taking a ministerial approach to their occupation in the larger society.

Youth ministry renews the church. Some of the most creative liturgies, catechetical programs, service projects, retreats, and faith experiences happen in youth ministry. Good youth ministry certainly renews the life of the faith community. And some young people who have been influenced by effective youth ministry will be the leaders of the church in many of its settings. They will push, pull, lead, or drag the church into a more inclusive and participative future. Youth ministry is, indeed, a hopeful activity.

Again, a Word of Caution

The promise of rich and rewarding payoffs might blind us to the myths encountered in working for the church and their being potential sources of conflict and frustration. So, again, here is a word of caution about them.

Keep in mind the following quote attributed to Thomas Merton. It was written specifically for those involved in the peace movement. However, if we substitute the word *youth minister* for *idealist* and *activist,* and the word *ministry* for *peace* (although *peace* reads very well also), Merton appears to be speaking to all of us involved in youth ministry, reminding us to maintain perspective and balance in our life and in our ministry.

> There is a pervasive form of violence to which the idealist [youth minister] fighting for peace [ministry with young people] by nonviolent methods most easily succumbs—activism and overwork.
> The rush and pressure of modern life are a form, perhaps the most common form, of its innate violence. To

allow oneself to be carried away by a multitude of conflicting concerns, to surrender to too many demands, to commit oneself to too many projects, to want to help everyone in everything is to succumb to violence.

More than that, it is cooperation in violence. The frenzy of the activist neutralizes one's work for peace. It destroys one's own inner capacity for peace. It destroys the fruitfulness of one's work, because it kills the root and inner wisdom which makes work fruitful.[1]

A Final Word of Encouragement

We must always remember why we are involved in youth ministry. We have responded to the Gospel challenge to serve, to witness, to build the Reign of God, and to proclaim the good news of Jesus. We will become frustrated. We will encounter obstacles, and some of these will be created by the very people we serve. But we are called to be faithful, not successful. The challenge is to be faithful to the Gospel. So hang in there! This is noble work that we do. It is the work of the Lord.

Reflection: And Now What?

① It's time to reflect on your situation.

a. In what ways have young people contributed to your personal, spiritual, and ministerial growth?

b. What is one of your "success" or "harvest" stories in youth ministry? Explain.

c. What have been the benefits or payoffs for you in youth ministry?

d. Reflect on the statement that we are called to be faithful, not successful. What are the practical implications for you of this claim?

2 Another way of taking stock of our ministry is to consider how we would describe this work to others. Complete the following ad for a youth minister:

YOUTH MINISTER NEEDED

In your next career, are you looking for _____
_____?

Do you have the gifts of _____
_____?

Do you want to enable young people to _____
_____?

Then an exciting career in youth ministry is for you! This is a challenging ministry because _____
_____?

And it requires a diversity of skills for _____
_____?

Not only will you touch the lives of young people for a lifetime, but the benefits for you include ___
_____ .

So now is the time . . . and this is the ministry!

---

3 It's also helpful to do a little gazing into the future, in order to get some perspective on the present. Complete the following sentences:

a. When I think about my ministry, my location, and my lifestyle, in five years I see myself _____
_____
_____

b. If I think I'll be in youth ministry, then the strategies I need to implement in order to continue to grow are
_____
_____

c. If I don't intend to stay in youth ministry, I should be preparing for the transition by _____
_____
_____

Endnotes

Introduction

1. Philip J. Murnion et al., *New Parish Ministers: Laity and Religious on Parish Staffs* (New York: National Pastoral Life Center, 1992), p. 52.

Chapter 1

1. Department of Education, United States Catholic Conference (USCC), *A Vision of Youth Ministry* (Washington, DC: USCC, 1986, ten-year anniversary edition).

2. National Federation for Catholic Youth Ministry (NFCYM) Committee on Certification and Accreditation, *NFCYM Competency-Based Standards for the Coordinator of Youth Ministry* (Washington, DC: NFCYM, 1990), p. vii.

3. John Roberto, "Toward Catholic Youth Ministry as a Profession," *NFCYM Connections*, Winter 1991, p. 1.

Chapter 3

1. Eugene C. Roehlkepartain, ed., *The Youth Ministry Resource Book* (Loveland, CO: Group Books, 1988), pp. 189–190, quoting an unpublished survey of 103 workers by Dr. Mark Lamport, Gordon College, Wenham, Massachusetts, 1987.

2. Murnion, *New Parish Ministers*, p. 93.

Chapter 4

1. Len Sperry, MD, "Determinants of a Minister's Well-Being," *Human Development*, Summer 1991, p. 24.

2. NFCYM et al., *The Challenge of Adolescent Catechesis: Maturing in Faith* (Washington, DC: NFCYM, 1986).

Chapter 5

1. Department of Education, USCC, *A Vision of Youth Ministry,* pp. 12–22.

Chapter 6

1. Doris Donnelly, keynote address at the Hofinger Conference, New Orleans, January 1991. Unpublished address.

2. Tilden Edwards, *Sabbath Time* (Nashville: Upper Room Books, 1992).

Chapter 7

1. NFCYM, "Ransoming the Time" (Washington, DC: NFCYM, August 1988, board meeting handout).